God loves me

Notes for parents or other adult readers

Sitting down to read a book with a young child is a special privilege, and helping them take early steps in getting to know their world, themselves and God is even more special. However this book is not just intended to be read, but to be a springboard for helping children learn throughout the day (Deuteronomy 6:4-7; Psalm 145:3-7). Here are a few tips to help you adapt your reading and help their learning go beyond these pages:

For really little ones: This book is intentionally repetitive to build key foundations. Reminding them of God's love through the day reinforces those foundations. Although they may not yet grasp how sending Jesus shows God's love, it's worth drawing the link and then building on it as they grow. (For more ideas, see the website.)

For bigger ones: Talk to them about God showing us his love by sending Jesus. As appropriate, start to explore questions like "Why did God send Jesus?" How can you help your child better understand God's love for them and how God wants us to respond to his love for us? (For more ideas, see the website.)

Other Bible passages to look at: Psalm 118:1; Psalm 145:8; John 3:16; Romans 5:8.

Making books for/with your child: Photograph your child at different times/places etc (or older children can draw). Drawings or a photo could be hung up with the caption 'God loves me'.

Pray: Regularly say short, simple prayers, like "Thank you God that you love me" and "Thank you God for Jesus".

For more details of these and other tips see www.teachinglittleones.com/bflo

Important note: The theme of 'God loves' is not as simple as it seems. Does God love sinners? If so, does that mean he accepts them? What sort of love is it? How do Jesus and faith fit in? And how does all this relate to young children? Space prevents us exploring these vital issues here. But we urge you to go to the website to read more.

Matthias Media (St Matthias Press Ltd ACN 067 558 365) Email: info@matthiasmedia.com.au
Internet: www.matthiasmedia.com Please visit our website for current postal and telephone contact information.

ISBN 978 1 922206 87 9

Cover design and typesetting by Karen Tse.

Photos: See www.teachinglittleones.com/bflo/photocredits.html

God made me and he loves me.
He loved me when I was a little baby.
He even loved me before I was born.

God loves me as I grow bigger...

...and bigger. He never stops loving me.

God loves me when I'm playing.

God loves me when I'm with my friends.

God loves me when I'm asleep.

And God loves me when I'm awake.
God loves me all day and all night.

God loves me all the time!

God loves me wherever I am.

God loves me when I'm happy.

God loves me when I'm sad.
God always loves me.

God's book, the Bible, says that
God showed us he loves us by sending Jesus.
Thank you God for Jesus!

"And God showed his love for us
by sending his only Son into the world."

1 John 4 verse 9

The name of God's Son is Jesus.

Thank you God that you love me lots and lots!